Communication
with
Your Child or Teen

MW00586207

ProActive
Parenting

FaithHome
for Parents

Abingdon Press

COMMUNICATION WITH YOUR CHILD OR TEEN
Copyright © 2004 by Abingdon Press

All rights reserved.
No part of this work may be reproduced or transmitted in any form or by any means, electronic or mechanical, including photocopying and recording, or by any information storage or retrieval system, except as may be expressly permitted by the 1976 Copyright Act or in writing from the publisher. Requests for permission should be addressed to Abingdon Press, P.O. Box 801, 201 Eighth Avenue South, Nashville, TN 37202-0801.

Scripture quotations noted NRSV are taken from the *New Revised Standard Version of the Bible*, copyright 1989 by the Division of Christian Education of the National Council of the Churches of Christ in the United States of America. Used by permission. All rights reserved.

Those noted NIV are from the *HOLY BIBLE, NEW INTERNATIONAL VERSION*®. Copyright © 1973, 1978, 1984 by International Bible Society. Used by permission of Zondervan Publishing House. All rights reserved.

Scripture taken from *THE MESSAGE* Copyright © Eugene H. Peterson, 1993, 1994, 1995. Used by permission of NavPress Publishing Group.

God's Word is a copyrighted work of God's Word to the Nations Bible Society. Quotations are used by permission. Copyright 1995 by God's Word to the Nations Bible Society. All rights reserved.

Parenting on Point: Leading Your Family Along God's Path by James C. Williams. Copyright 2002 by Abingdon Press, Nashville, Tennessee, 37202. Reprinted by permission.

04 05 06 07 08 09 10 11 12 13—10 9 8 7 6 5 4 3 2 1

MANUFACTURED IN THE UNITED STATES OF AMERICA

Contents

Contents

Everything You Need to Know Before You Begin This Study

According to Stephen Covey, author of *The Seven Habits of Highly Effective People,* we have a choice: We can live either in a circle of concern or a circle of influence. When we live in a circle of concern, we're always reacting to events and circumstances. We fail to plan or prepare or look ahead. Often we end up "putting out fires" and racing from one crisis to another. When we live in a circle of influence, on the other hand, we're always one step ahead. Planning and preparation are part of our everyday lives. We know our desired goal, and we plan accordingly in order to achieve it. The *ProActive Parenting* series is about choosing to live in a circle of influence—with God in the center. Simply put, it is about learning how to parent with a plan so that you can become the kind of parent that God wants you to be.

Communication with Your Child or Teen is intended to help you improve your relationships with your children by helping you to improve your communication with your children and set a godly example in your home. This brings us to two concepts that are foundational to this study as well as the entire *ProActive Parenting* series.

Two Key Concepts

1. The North Star Versus the Artificial Star

Jim Williams, parenting expert, author, and video presenter of this series, says that parenting is similar to navigating: You need an unchanging reference point such as the North Star to help keep you on course. In his book *Parenting on Point,* he explains that this North Star is the moral center of the family, or the core beliefs, values, and principles that help your family to stay on the course God wants you to follow. As Christian parents, your North Star will include biblical beliefs and values—such as those found in the Ten Commandments (Deuteronomy 5:6-21), the Golden Rule (Matthew 7:12), the new commandment of Jesus (Matthew 22:37-40), and the love chapter (1 Corinthians 13)—as well as other important principles that support and strengthen the family.

One of your most important parenting responsibilities is to identify and communicate your North Star. In fact, Jim Williams says that you must *clearly articulate* your North Star if you want to keep your children from being pulled "off course" by an even larger, more magnetic star called the artificial star. The artificial star represents the values of popular culture. It is the cultural ethos that encourages your children to …

- ◆ Do what feels good (rather than do what's right)
- ◆ Pursue instant gratification (rather than practice delayed gratification)
- ◆ Look out for "number one" (rather than live the Golden Rule)

Regrettably, the artificial star is bigger today than ever before, and it continues to grow at an exponential rate thanks to the entertainment industry. If you want your children to follow your family's North Star, rather than be pulled off course by the huge artificial star, then you must be proactive in identifying and clearly communicating your values to your children.

2. The Family Mission Statement

One of the most effective ways to communicate your family's values is by writing a family mission statement. If you have already written a family mission statement, then you will want to review it and make any necessary revisions. If you have not already written a family mission statement, then you will begin working on one during Week 1 of this study (see the step-by-step guidelines provided on pages 19-20). Jim Williams encourages you to involve your children in the process, explaining, "If you want your children to 'catch' the core family values, which are reflected in the family mission statement, then they need to feel they are involved in the process of creating that statement" (*Parenting on Point,* p. 37). If your children are not yet in elementary school, their participation and understanding naturally will be limited. Still, even young children can participate in writing a simple mission statement based on the Golden Rule (Matthew 7:12) or the new commandment of Jesus (Matthew 22:37-40).

The process of writing a family mission statement will take several weeks. Set a goal for completion and schedule at least two family "sessions" prior to this date when you may work on it together. You might consider having one or more of these family sessions in a weekend getaway at a hotel, campground, or other setting. This will turn what otherwise might be a dreaded exercise into a fun family experience. However you choose to do it, writing a family mission statement will be an incredibly rewarding exercise that will help to build a strong foundation for your family for many years to come.

Now that you have a basic understanding of what *ProActive Parenting* is all about, let's move on to the basics of how each study works.

A Quick Overview

This four-week study has been designed to be easy to use. The material for each week is divided into three sections: Before Class, During Class, and After Class. In the first section you will find brief background material, called Background Basics, which will prepare you for the group session. You will be able to complete each reading in just a few minutes. Please don't skip this important step. Some of the material included here will not be covered in class and will give you additional information that will be beneficial both during and after the group session.

The second section walks you through the one-hour group session, which consists primarily of video segments and group discussion. Jim Williams, a dynamic parenting instructor, will be your "guest speaker" each week. To help you "get acquainted" with Jim, be sure to read the compelling story of why he is so passionate about helping you to become a proactive parent (see pages 9-10).

After viewing the first two video segments, you will have the opportunity to discuss several questions that will allow you to share your own thoughts and ideas as well as benefit from others' insights and experiences. If your group has no time constraints, you may want to extend this discussion time, lengthening the total time of the group session. There simply is no substitute for the encouragement and support of other parents whose family values and goals are in line with your own. In fact, you may find your group experience to be so valuable that you will want to do another study in this series together, or choose to continue meeting informally as a parenting support group.

Prayer and scripture are two valuable components of every group session as well. The group facilitator may choose to use the opening and closing prayers provided or create original prayers. In either case, the intent is to "cover" the group session in prayer, acknowledging that we are incapable of being the parents God wants us to be without God's grace, strength, and help. Likewise, the "Wisdom from the Word" provided for each group session is intended not only to provide a biblical foundation for the group session, but also to highlight relevant verses that you may meditate on throughout the week. Take time each day to read and reflect on the Wisdom from the Word for that week, asking God to show you how these truths apply to your own family life. Hebrews 4:12 tells us that "the word of God is living and active" (NRSV). Likewise, we read in Isaiah 55:11, "My word…shall not return to me empty, but it shall accomplish that which I purpose, and succeed in the thing for which I sent it" (NRSV). If you will seek God's guidance through the Holy Scriptures, you can *expect* to receive the direction and wisdom you desire!

The third and final section of each week's material offers Homework exercises and Tools and Tips that will help you with the practical step of application. Don't let the word "homework" scare you! You will not be asked to "turn in" these exercises or share any details with the group. They are intended for your private use and your family's benefit only.

They are not intended, however, to be "optional." Each exercise is designed to help you get the most out of this study that you possibly can. Whether or not this is just another parenting class or a transformational learning experience that will have a lasting, positive impact on you and your family is up to you. So you are strongly encouraged to complete as much of the Homework assignments as you can each week and to use those Tools and Tips that are applicable to your family. If you do, you will be well on your way to becoming a proactive parent—a parent who chooses to live in a circle of influence with God in the center.

Introducing Jim Williams

God brings special people into our lives to instruct and encourage us along life's journey, and often these people help to change our lives in ways we never could have anticipated. Jim Williams is one of those special people for me and for many, many other parents who have had the privilege of taking one of his parenting courses. One thing that makes Jim so special is that he's not just another "parenting expert." He is a disciple of Jesus Christ who has a God-given mission to help families "get back on track"—on the path that God wants them to follow. Jim's story is best told in his own words. So I invite you to get comfortable and "listen" with both your head and your heart as Jim shares why he is so passionate about helping you to become a better parent—a proactive parent who strives to keep God in the center of your family's life.

Sally Sharpe
Series Editor

My life changed forever on November 11, 1995, when a drunk driver killed my nineteen-year-old son, Curt. That night I came to the full realization that God gives everyone the free will to choose. That night a man exercised his free will to choose, and he chose to drink and then drive his truck home while intoxicated. My world was shattered.

At the time, Curt was a sophomore at Birmingham-Southern College, where he was thriving. Meanwhile, back at home, I was having great difficulty enjoying the parenting experience with my sixteen-year-old daughter, Beth. I was frustrated because she did not "embrace my world" as I thought she should, and we fought all the time.

When the call came from the hospital in Birmingham on the night of Curt's accident, my wife, Carol, left immediately, and I waited to locate Beth, who was out on a date. A few hours later, Beth and I rode all the way to Birmingham without even talking. I sat in the front seat with my minister, and Beth sat in the backseat by herself.

Two days after Curt's funeral, God "opened my eyes." I realized for the first time how distant Beth and I had become. I realized that I needed to change as a parent or I was going to lose Beth, too.

Approximately six months after Curt's death, I was advised by my employer of twenty-three years that my business unit was being eliminated and I was losing

my job. This action gave me the opportunity to reevaluate my life's work. The fact that this loss happened so soon after the loss of Curt helped to "open my ears" and enabled me to listen to God. I felt that God was leading me to make a difference in the lives of children and parents by combining my life-long passion for outreach with my recent volunteer work for STARS (Students Taking a Right Stand), a nonprofit organization in the public school system whose mission is to help children make healthy lifestyle choices. So, with incredible support from my family and my peers, I worked to develop a series of educational and motivational speeches and classroom presentations for children, followed by a series of parenting classes and workshops for adults. Ever since, I have been working full-time in the classroom, devoting my days to helping children and my evenings to helping parents.

After continued requests from parents for a printed copy of my "teachings," God engineered circumstances making it possible for the book Parenting on Point *to be born. Now this study series,* ProActive Parenting, *makes it possible for me to reach even more parents via video each week, sharing practical insights on how they can keep God in the center of their lives despite the negative influence of popular culture. There's no limit to what God can do—and that includes what God can do for your family through this study.*

I hope that as you view the video segments each week, you will feel as if we have become friends. As I share my life and the insights I have gained through personal and professional experience, study, and various mentors, my hope is that you will take away better skills to meet the many challenges you face as a parent, and that you will be motivated to use these skills in your daily life. If you do, I promise that not only will you enjoy the parenting experience far more than I did, but also, through a commitment to ProActive Parenting and a renewed commitment to your children, you will find it easier to be the parent that God wants you to be.

Jim Williams

Recognizing the Barriers We Build

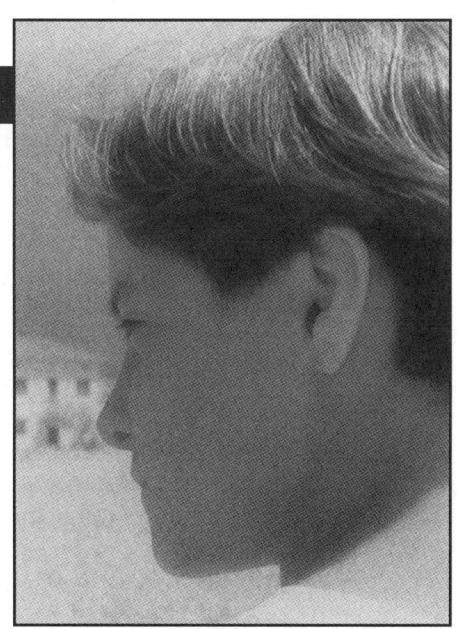

Before Class

Background Basics

Proactive parents know that effective communication is crucial to successful parenting because communication is the glue that holds the parent-child relationship together. This study is designed to help you improve your relationships with your children by helping you to improve your communication with your children. Because our children model our behavior, we begin our study this week by looking at how *we* communicate.

The Need to Be Understood

Why is it so difficult for us to be good listeners? In his book *The Seven Habits of Highly Effective Families,* Stephen Covey reintroduces Maslow's Hierarchy of Needs, explaining that the top three needs that motivate human behavior are safety/security, food, and clothing. He then explains that, for most of us, these needs are usually met and, therefore, do not motivate our behavior on a daily basis. On down the list, however, is a need that Covey believes drives our behavior, especially when it comes to communicating. It is the need to be understood. If we're not careful, this need can become one of the biggest barriers to being a good listener.

We all have the need to be understood. If you question this, then the next time someone begins talking to you, count how many seconds pass before you begin formulating a response in your mind! Generally, it's less than 10-15 seconds. And if the person speaking has a loud tone or is demonstrating body language that communicates anger or conflict, we begin mentally formulating our defense almost instantly. Why do we do this? Because we have the need to be understood. Before we can become good listeners, we must "reprogram" our brains, which requires us to recognize those "bad behaviors" that keep us from learning to understand others before seeking to be understood.

Problem Personalities

Let's consider some of the common "bad behaviors" or habits we perpetuate that keep us from seeking to understand others. The Johnson Institute has identified several "problem personalities" that we habitually take on when we're trying to listen to our children, which act as barriers to effective communication. In his book *Parenting on Point* (pp. 132-133), Jim Williams briefly describes each personality:

The Drill Sergeant doesn't care what the child has to say and, instead of listening, barks out orders.

The Prosecuting Attorney asks a number of aggressive and penetrating questions in order to determine whether or not the child is at fault, which consequently makes the child feel that he or she *is* at fault.

The Psychiatrist tells the child how he or she feels and why, before even allowing the child to tell his or her story.

The Comedian makes fun of the child's situation or feelings.

The Egomaniac shifts the focus from the child to self.

The Avoider changes the subject or leaves the room. (Sadly, many of the fifth and sixth grade students that Williams works with say they have difficulty talking to their parents because they're always too busy—which is perceived as avoiding them.)

These personalities have one thing in common: a lack of concern for the child's feelings. Williams suggests that this insensitivity is the result of wearing what he calls our "sunglasses."

Our "Sunglasses"

Our "sunglasses" represent all of our life experiences that prejudice us towards others' points of view, thereby shading what we hear them saying. Our sunglasses ...

◆ prevent us from seeing things through others' eyes.
◆ keep our focus on ourselves rather than on others.
◆ make it very difficult to express our love and care for others.

According to Williams, we wear our sunglasses when we give our children the "third degree" by bombarding them with questions or when we express our feelings before giving them a chance to express theirs. On the other hand, he says that we take off our sunglasses when we truly hear and understand our children's world, intentionally expressing our genuine love and care through our words, our body language, and our actions (*Parenting on Point,* p. 139). Though it takes time to break the habit of wearing our sunglasses, it can be done over time if we're intentional and persistent.

Ineffective Listening Habits

In addition to wearing our sunglasses, there are several ineffective listening habits that Stephen Covey says can keep us from being effective communicators with our children. First, we often become *selective listeners.* If we're interested in what our children want to talk about, we listen; if not, we ignore what they say. Jim Williams says that if the topic is high on our priority list or interests us personally, we eagerly listen, but if the subject is boring or makes us feel uncomfortable, we eagerly "tune out" and avoid contributing to the conversation. Second, we sometimes become *pretend listeners*, mumbling pat responses such as "Yes," "No," and "Uh huh" while our minds are somewhere else.

As Williams confesses, he learned the hard way that each of these poor listening habits can boomerang on us, causing our children to practice the very same poor listening habits with us! After all, our children model our behavior. This is why identifying some of the barriers *we* build is such an important step in improving communication in our homes.

"Bridges" to Effective Communication

The Family Mission Statement

In addition to identifying the barriers that keep you from being an effective communicator in your home, it is important to identify the "bridges" that can help you to bring about positive change. One of the most effective bridges you can build is a family mission statement based on your family's core values.

A recurring theme of the *ProActive Parenting* series is the importance of identifying your family's core values—what Jim Williams calls your family's "North Star." He says that just as navigators of years past used the North Star to guide their vessels and reach their intended destinations, so also your family needs a "North Star" to help keep you on the right course. In his book *Parenting on Point,* he explains that this North Star is the moral center of the family, or the core beliefs, values, and principles that help your family to stay on the course God wants you to follow. As Christian parents, your North Star will include biblical beliefs and values—such as those found in the Ten Commandments (Deuteronomy 5:6-21), the Golden Rule (Matthew 7:12), the new commandment of Jesus (Matthew 22:37-40), and the love chapter (1 Corinthians 13)—as well as other important principles that support and strengthen the family such as forgiveness, family worship, servanthood, family time and family fun, fairness, and active listening.

One of your most important parenting responsibilities is identifying and communicating your North Star in a family mission statement. If you have already written a family mission statement, perhaps as part of another study in this series, review it and make any revisions or additions if necessary. If you have not yet written a family mission statement, you are strongly encouraged to begin this process with your children this week. If you want your children to "catch" your values and understand the connection between those values and the ways family members are expected to communicate in your home, then they need to have ownership in your family mission statement. One of your Homework assignments this week will be to complete the first step in writing a family mission statement (see pages 19-20), which is identifying your core values.

The S-P-E-A-K Strategy

Another helpful "bridge" to effective communication is the S-P-E-A-K strategy. Experts recommend this helpful tool for "checking" our own behavior and communication habits. Each letter reminds us of a separate action or step necessary for good communication with our children:

S – Speak the truth in love.
P – Permit all feelings to be expressed.
E – Educate yourself about your child's developmental stages.
A – Actively listen.
K – Know your children and yourself.

(*Talking with Your Child: Conversations for Life,* Rebecca Laird, editor, Nashville: Abingdon Press: 1999, p. 6)

We will address the "E"—educate yourself about your child's developmental stages—in Week 2 as we discuss the ages and stages of children, and the "K"—know your children and yourself—in Week 3 as we discuss differences in our communication "styles." The remaining steps will be covered in Week 4 as we explore some of the specific ways you can improve communication in your home.

During Class

In Focus

The purpose of this session is to identify some of the common barriers we build that keep us from being good listeners at home, and to consider ways we can bring about change in our own communication habits so that our children will want to model our own positive example.

Wisdom from the Word

"Your ears are open but you don't hear a thing." (Matthew 13:14 The Message)

Opening Prayer

Dear God, we admit that we're not always good listeners, and that we must be willing to change if we expect our children to become good listeners. Give us wisdom and understanding today so that we may identify the ways you are calling each us to change our own listening habits. May we tear down the barriers we have allowed to come between us and our children and begin to build bridges leading to improved communication. Amen.

Video Segment 1

Candid Kids

Running Time: 1:57 minutes

Discussion Questions

1. Did you gain any insights from the children's comments?
2. Was there one comment that caught your attention more than others?

Video Segment 2

A Parent's Perspective

Running Time: 17:46 minutes

Group Discussion

1. Read aloud this week's Wisdom from the Word (page 15). Jim Williams says the number one reason we fail to hear what others are saying is that we begin formulating a response while they are talking. Why do

we do this? (Be as specific as you can.) What can we learn from Matthew 19:19b regarding the mindset or attitude we should have when communicating with others?

2. What do you think is the primary downfall or danger of each of the five "problem personalities" discussed in the video (drill sergeant, prosecuting attorney, psychiatrist, comedian, egomaniac)?

3. Of the three "listening levels" discussed in the video, in which level do you tend to fall most often? (avoider, pretend listener, selective listener)? Why?

Video Segment 3

In Summary

Running Time: 0:50 minutes

Closing Prayer

Lord, thank you for this time of learning and fellowship. Thank you for the insights you've given us related to the barriers that keep us from being good listeners and the bridges we need to build. Help us to apply what we've learned as we communicate with our children this week, and to complete our homework assignments for next time. Amen.

After Class

Homework

1. Discuss the class session. What new insight(s) or understanding(s) did you gain? What do you believe will be of greatest benefit to you/your family?

_____

_____

2. Pay close attention to your listening habits with your children this week. Which of the "problem personalities" (p. 12) and ineffective listening habits (p. 13) do you most often exhibit?

_____

_____

Why do you think this is so?

_____

_____

_____

Work on "reprogramming" your response, remembering to "take off your sunglasses" and truly hear and understand what is being said.

3. Review the "Four Commandments of Communication" included in Tools and Tips (page 18). Which of these "commandments" is most difficult for you to keep and why?

_____

_____

_____

Focus on this commandment this week, and pay attention to how it helps to improve communication in your home.

4. Try to catch yourself in a couple of "conversation stoppers" this week (see page 19), and change your normal response. Post a copy on the refrigerator or another highly visible place as a reminder.

5. Because all of the communication in your home should support your family's core values, it is important to identify and express these values in a family mission statement. If you have not already written a mission statement for your family, begin working on one following the instructions in Tools and Tips. Remember that it will require several weeks to complete your family mission statement. Complete step #1 this week, making notes in the space below, and schedule times on your calendar for completing the remaining steps. If possible, make plans for a fun family getaway where you can have a brainstorming session, write a first draft, and enjoy time together. Set a target completion date for your finished statement.

These are the core values and beliefs that are central to keeping our family on the right path:

_____

_____

_____

_____

6. Read the Background Basics for Week 2.

Tools and Tips

The Four Commandments of Communication

Commandment 1.   LISTEN MORE.
What you hear is always more important than what you say. Become a careful listener; talk less.

Commandment 2.   TELL THE TRUTH.
Building trust with your children is based on telling the truth.

Commandment 3.   ALLOW ALL FEELINGS TO BE EXPRESSED.
Let your children tell you how they feel. Help them direct their frustration, anger, or disappointment to the real issue or circumstance.

Commandment 4.   RECOGNIZE YOUR OWN DEFENSIVENESS.

What in your child really sets you off? Do you resort to defensive tactics like sarcasm or stonewalling? Are some of these "hot buttons" related to your own experience with your parents? Learn what makes you uncomfortable so that you can respond better to your child rather than react to your own experiences.
(Adapted from *Talking with Your Teen: Conversations for Life*, Lynn Hutton, editor, Nashville: Abingdon Press, 1999, p.6)

Conversation Stoppers

Blaming: "If you would have gotten yourselves out of bed when I first called this morning, we wouldn't be late!"

Shaming: "I don't know what is wrong with you kids! No matter what I do, you don't seem to get yourselves going in the morning!"

Explaining: "I didn't get involved in your bathroom fight this morning because you have to learn to take care of yourselves sometimes. Joe, you take too long in the shower. Julia, you have to pick out your clothes the night before. Why, when I was a kid, I had to arrive at the breakfast table with my clothes on and hair combed."

Defensiveness: "It's not my fault you're going to be late. Don't expect me to give your choir director any excuses for you."

Stonewalling: "I don't want to hear a word out of either of you this morning!"

Exaggerating: "You kids always make me late. You never try to get places on time. You don't care if your whole choir has to wait for you two."

(Adapted from *Talking with Your Child: Conversations for Life,* Rebecca Laird, editor, Nashville: Abingdon Press, 1999, p. 10)

How to Write a Family Mission Statement

1. Identify and discuss those things that are central to your ability to keep your family headed in the right direction. This includes, but is not limited to, your core values and beliefs.
2. As a family, have a brainstorming session around these topics. Allow family members to add ideas of their own without critique. "No idea is a bad idea."
3. Work together to identify core ideas and common threads.
4. Put the core ideas and common threads into salient points. This is your first draft.
5. Post your first draft, or give each family member a copy, and "let it simmer" for a while.
6. Review your mission statement together as a family.
7. Make revisions and finalize it.
8. Print it, frame it, and hang it.

Next steps...

1. Identify core commitments that will enable you to live out your mission statement (e.g., a commitment to a moral framework, church involvement, family time, a healthy lifestyle, a family budget, etc.).
2. Write a list of yearly family goals and objectives based on your core commitments; print them and post them.

(Adapted from *Parenting on Point,* pp. 48-49)

Understanding Ages and Stages

Before Class

Background Basics

Last week we looked at some of the barriers we create that keep us from being good listeners, and we considered a couple of "bridges" that can help us to bring about positive change. That's an important first step in becoming better communicators with our children. Now we're ready to shift our focus to our children and the ways they communicate with us.

Although all children are continually developing their own communication skills, there are specific changes or abilities that can be observed at certain ages. If we want to be proactive parents, we must become familiar with these developmental stages so that we may be intentional about the ways we interact with our children.

Early Childhood

The preschool years are a wonderful time. We enjoy watching our little ones learn to walk and talk, seeing their new discoveries, and playing with them. But these years also are a time for us to begin developing a method of communication with our children that fosters relationships and personal growth. Let's take a look at some of the developmental skills that can be observed in these years.

Two-year-olds can understand and sometimes talk about things that can be seen and touched using short phrases, though much of what a child this age says is still unintelligible. Talk with your child even when the conversation is one-sided. Your child will respond more and more as your conversations continue. The more you talk, the better! They understand the concept of me and mine, yet they are not able to share. Remember that two-year-olds are experiencing frustration as they want to do more things for themselves but aren't capable. It's a time of transition between infancy and early childhood, and emotional upheavals are to be expected.

Three-year-olds can communicate using full sentences, and nearly all of what they say is understandable. They can tell you their names, ages, and genders, and they understand the concepts of *in, on,* and *under.* Three's are beginning to have opinions, and they respond best to simple, limited choices. Ask "yes" or "no" questions, and offer choices that you can live with regardless of which option your child chooses.

Four-year-olds are able to communicate with words and actions, becoming more and more capable of expressing thoughts and feelings. They know the names of animals, objects in the home, and some colors. Often they talk out loud, narrating as they play. A four-year-old can share, but can't yet explain behavior or control it at all times. Fours may even think you can read their minds, and may be confused when you don't understand them. Encourage your child to talk in short but complete sentences, and respond in a similar way.

Five-year-olds are capable of following simple instructions with only a few steps (e.g., "Take your clothes off, put them in the hamper, and put on your pajamas"). They are beginning to discern simple emotions and differentiate the passage of time (yesterday, tomorrow, this weekend). Talk with your child about his or her morning, teacher, favorite foods, and so forth. This is a creative, participatory age when your child will enjoy talking with you.

The Elementary School Years

During the elementary school years—ages 6-12—our children have three primary communication issues: security, predictability, and responsibility.

Security. Tell your child how safe he or she is, and explain the types of protections that are in place to ensure that safety. Reassure your child regularly of your love.

Predictability. Stay as consistent as possible in your language, expectations, and schedules. Having structure and knowing what to expect are important for children this age.

Responsibility. Begin to help your child be responsible for his or her words and actions. Take the lead by demonstrating that your "yes" means "yes" and your "no" means "no."

In addition, there are two important developmental characteristics that surface during these years that can dramatically affect the way our children communicate: aggressive emotions and sassy behavior.

Aggressive emotions. It's normal for elementary school children to begin dealing more often with emotions that can trigger aggressive behavior, such as jealousy and anger—especially in their relationships with friends. Talk with your child about his or her feelings and help your child to channel those feelings in productive ways.

Sassy behavior. As your child approaches the fifth or sixth grade and begins preparing for the independence of adolescence, you can expect a little more assertive behavior. He or she may begin to question you or ask for explanations in a new way. Try to distinguish between times when your child is speaking his or her mind and times when your child is showing disrespect. Remember that it's not really disrespectful for a child to ask, "Why do I have to do this?"

With these generalities in mind, let's take a brief look at some of the milestones or "markers" of the elementary years.

Six-year-olds are able to follow lengthy verbal instructions, and they can do more involved tasks such as making a sandwich or sorting laundry. Sixes understand opposites, can tell time using a clock, and can tell a complete story with a beginning, middle, and end. Be encouraging as your child begins to express his or her own ideas and individual personality.

Seven-year-olds can express their feelings well with words. They can read and write many words and categorize things that are alike and different. At this age they also begin feeling a little insecure about their place in social settings. Reassure your child by affirming his or her new abilities and emerging personality.

Eight-year-olds like to please and are eager to discuss good-and-bad and right-and-wrong. They can tell you details of events (how the teacher explained something) or subjects (the parts of a flower or the characteristics of an animal), write simple reports, and comfortably initiate conversations with peers and trusted adults. Be available and interested whenever your child is eager to talk.

Nine-year-olds are active dynamos who want the world to be fair. They are prone to making checklists and enjoy classifying and ordering information. Nines can read lengthy books, write reports, and understand and discuss some world events. Talk about current events with your child on an appropriate level and be prepared to answer questions.

Ten-year-olds are usually comfortable with their parents and peers in social settings and enjoy trying new skills and games. By this age, a child's verbal abilities are highly developed. This also is the age when anger, often unexpected and fierce, can surface. Remember that anger is common at this age, and help your child to express and channel his or her feelings in productive ways.

Eleven-year-olds are outgoing and communicate as "adolescents in training." Most are slow to comply and quick to criticize their mothers. They are fond of arguing and often ask for explanations in new ways as well as exhibit sassy behavior. Remember that your child's questions and argumentative behavior may not signal disrespect but rather an immature attempt at speaking his or her mind.

Twelve-year-olds are eager to talk and generally enthusiastic. Angry outbursts begin to decrease at this age, yet twelves continue to like to argue a point. They are beginning to become more tolerant of their parents and begin to experiment with personal choices, especially those pertaining to their personal appearance and activities with friends. Allow your child to exercise his or her increasing responsibility and regularly affirm your child with words and actions.

The Teen Years

As your child enters the teen years, you will notice increasing anxiety about continuing physical changes—such as changes in height, voice, complexion, body shape, and sexual development. Generally speaking, teenage girls are more mature in their sexuality than teenage boys. You may notice that your daughter is gaining a little weight and becoming taller than some of the boys in their class. Your son may be eating a great deal and developing stronger body odor. These kinds of changes often make teens feel awkward and self-conscious. Let's look at more detailed descriptions of the teen years and consider some communication tips.

Thirteen-year-olds are particularly sensitive to the physical changes they are experiencing, which is why it is so important to remain sensitive to their feelings and regularly encourage them about their appearance and new activities. It's important not to tease your teen about these changes—even in good-natured joking. He or she gets enough of that at school! Remember that your teen's self-perception is largely reflected by you. Fathers, particularly, can help their daughters to have good self-esteem by being supportive and encouraging of their physical appearance. Compliment your daughter on her appearance. Give her hugs and reassurance.

Fourteen- and fifteen-year-olds can be moody and have more conflicts with their friends. Girls may begin to have daily arguments with their mothers about clothes, curfews, friends, and makeup Boys often "detach," spending more time alone in their rooms or out with friends. This is the time for you to use "I feel" statements (I respect..., I love..., I enjoy..., or It makes me uncomfortable...) rather than "you" statements. "I" statements describe your own feelings or concerns rather than making judgments about your teen. They reflect your own position and perspective on a situation. This kind of approach will help you to get your teen's feelings out. As your teen talks to you about certain activities and events, ask how they make your teen feel. Also, be a resource for your teen rather than a problem solver. Your teen needs your help in learning how to solve problems independently, without you trying to solve them instead (see the "Six-Step Problem Solving Method" provided on page 32). This will help to build your teen's confidence.

Sixteen-, seventeen- and eighteen-year-olds are preparing for high school graduation and desire even more independence. Now they can drive and can get away from you for extended periods of time. At times they may show disinterest in former or prior interests; this is normal. They'll also want to make their own choices in critical areas such as school and church. Some teens this age feel invincible and show a disregard for personal safety. Without allowing your teen to make reckless choices, do let your teen experiment with freedom and learn from *safe* mistakes. As your maturing teen takes on more and more responsibilities, remember to expand his or her boundaries; and continue listening to your teen's frustrations without trying to solve his or her problems.

Empowering Your Child

There's a common need that crosses over all the age groups of our children, and if we address this need properly, we will strengthen the communication lines with our children. If we address it poorly, however, we will weaken the communication lines. It is the need for empowerment. Empowering our children is simply the act of allowing them to learn from their mistakes. It's the idea that we're going to give them responsibilities and then hold them accountable, helping them to see that mistakes and failures are lessons, not judgments on their worth. As parents, we must realize that we cannot guarantee our children's success, but we can equip them to face failure with courage and character.

Many parents, unfortunately, enable their children rather than empower them. They step in before the child has an opportunity to make a choice. In their book *Parenting with Love and Logic,* Dr. Foster Cline and Jim Fay explain that parents easily become what they call helicopter parents— parents who hover over their children and then swoop down and keep them from making a bad decision or choice. In time, those children start avoiding their parents because they don't want them to solve all their problems for them, and thus the lines of communication begin to weaken. If parents are not careful, their enabling habits can actually create a "rebel," which is a child who rebels against the family values and *never comes back to them.*

What, then, are some specific ways we can empower, rather than enable, our children?

- Celebrate each of your children for who he or she is without making comparisons, and treat each child as an individual.
- Help your children to discover and develop their God-given gifts and abilities. (Identify and communicate both skills and characteristics you see in your children.)
- Offer specific and appropriate praise for good behavior and accomplishments. (Avoid exaggerated praise.)
- Let your children work out their differences, acting as a mediator only when necessary or appropriate.
- Discourage competition and comparison among your children.
- When your children make a mistake or have a problem, be a resource rather than the solution, walking them through the six-step problem solving method (see p. 32).
- Soothe your children's hurt when they fail by
    - helping them look ahead
    - relating a story of someone you know
    - talking it over
    - relating a story of your own failure
    - reading or telling stories about famous people who failed
    - evaluating the situation and identifying "lessons"

(Adapted from Talking with Your Child: Conversations for Life, Rebecca Laird, ed., Abingdon Press, 1999, pp. 29-32.)

In these and other ways we can choose to empower our children rather than enable them. Through *all* the ages and stages, empowering our children is a great way to keep the lines of communication open while helping our children to build self-confidence and self-esteem.

During Class

In Focus

The purpose of this session is to remind you that children develop communication skills at differing rates, and to help you recognize some of the common changes or abilities that can be observed at various ages and stages of growth.

Wisdom from the Word

When I was a child, I spoke like a child, I thought like a child, I reasoned like a child; when I became an adult, I put an end to childish ways. (1 Corinthians 13:11 NRSV)

Opening Prayer

Dear God, thank you for the precious gift of our children. Too often our unrealistic or unmet expectations lead to frustration and conflict in our homes, causing a breakdown in communication. We desire to understand our children better and, therefore, to communicate with them more effectively. Open our own ears today, Lord, so that we will be good listeners. Amen.

Video Segment 1

Candid Kids

Running Time: 1:31 minutes

Discussion Questions

1. Did you gain any insights from the children's comments?
2. Was there one comment that caught your attention more than others?

Video Segment 2

A Parent's Perspective

Running Time: 15:15 minutes

Group Discussion

1. Read aloud this week's Wisdom from the Word (page 26). How can understanding the specific communication skills and abilities that can be observed at different ages help us to improve our communication with our children? Give an example, if possible.
2. Discuss the inverted triangle approach to parenting presented in the video. Why is it important to increase a child's responsibilities and privileges as the child matures and earns your trust? What is the danger of unfairly restricting a child's boundaries in the teen years?
3. What does it mean to live in a circle of influence, rather than a circle of concern? What insights have you gained this week that will help you to be proactive, rather than reactive, as you communicate with your children?

In Summary

Running Time: 0:36 minutes

Closing Prayer
Lord, thank you for this time of learning and fellowship. Thank you for the insights you've given us related to the different communication abilities and stages of children. Help us to apply what we've learned as we communicate with our children this week and complete our homework assignments for next time. Amen.

After Class

Homework
1. Discuss the class session. What new insight(s) or understanding(s) did you gain? What do you believe will be of greatest benefit to you/your family?

_____

_____

2. Review the developmental stage(s) of your child/ren. Do these descriptions seem to fit? Why or why not? What is your greatest communication challenge with each of your children?

_____

_____

_____

_____

3. Try some of the age-appropriate tips for communicating including in Tools and Tips (page 29-32), and note the results as well as any insights you gain.

Tip	Result/Insight
_____	_____
_____	_____
_____	_____
_____	_____
_____	_____
_____	_____

4. Review and discuss the suggestions for empowering your children (p. 26), and brainstorm some specific ways you can apply these strategies in your family:

_____

_____

_____

_____

5. Read the Background Basics for Week 3.

Tools and Tips

Tips for Communicating with Young Children

1. Be aware of opportunities for talking to and with your preschooler while you're "on the go"—driving in the car, working or playing around the house, or even walking from the car to the store.
2. Set aside at least fifteen minutes each day as uninterrupted time for you and your child to talk about the day. Talk about specific moments and what made him or her happy, sad, afraid, or mad.
3. Talk about concrete things in your child's world, including sights, sounds, smells, colors, and textures.
4. Offer choices. Try saying, "Would you like a hot dog or soup?" instead of "What would you like to eat?"

5. Ask your child to repeat any instructions that he or she doesn't understand. Keep in mind that generally preschoolers cannot remember a series of instructions.
6. Demonstrate appropriate manners with your own language and behavior.
7. Sit with your child at bedtime as he or she prays aloud.
8. Read together and talk about the story; this is an excellent way to help build communication skills.
9. Discuss your child's fears (e.g., "There's a monster in my closet") rather than dismiss them ("There's no such thing as monster"), and give your child helps for handling those fears (give your child a flashlight or look in the closet together).
10. Seek help if your child
    ◆ does not respond to his or her name unless you are making eye contact.
    ◆ does not react to loud noises, even when they are in close range.
    ◆ consistently struggles to articulate simple words, particularly those with beginning or ending consonants.
    ◆ continues baby talk after age five.

(Adapted from "Communicating with Your Preschooler," FaithHome for Parents, Carolyn Johnson, Abingdon Press, 1999, pp. 4-6.)

Tips for Communicating with Children in the Elementary School Years

1. Answer all questions, and answer honestly—even if the answer is "I don't know" or "Let me think about it."
2. If you're unclear about your child's question, restate it.
3. Don't make promises you can't keep. Try to be realistic in your plans.
4. Don't be surprised to hear "I hate you" and other angry comments. Encourage your child to rail at the boundaries rather than at you.
5. Take time to talk about the details of your child's day. Your child may tell rambling stories, but he or she still needs your time and attention.
6. Develop a "secret sign" that the two of you can share silently whenever you want to say "I need to talk with you."
7. Be the driver. Whenever possible, provide transportation for your child and his or her friends. You may learn a great deal more about their interests and concerns from their energetic conversations in the backseat than you would from a direct question.
8. Be as clear as possible about desired behavior changes or concerns without being negative about your child and his or her personality or ability.

9. Don't solve your child's problems; instead, help your child learn the six-step problem solving method (see p. 32).
10. Seek help if...
    ♦ your child has regular, uncontrollable emotional outbursts or mood swings.
    ♦ your child has threatened to harm self or others.
    ♦ your child's actions or words regularly interfere with social, academic, or family development.
    ♦ your child's behaviors are continually disruptive to the family.
    ♦ your child avoids school, or has frequent headaches or stomachaches that keep him or her from school. (Look for triggers that may be causing this reaction.)

(Adapted from "Communicating with Your Child Ages 6-12," "FaithHome for Parents, Tony Rankin and Cynthia Ezell, Abingdon Press, 1999, pp.3-6)

Tips for Communicating with Teens

1. Think about your own teen years and your relationship with your parents during that time. Areas that were important to you may be particularly important to you now as hopes for your child. Be aware of these areas, and keep in mind that your child may not be as concerned about them as you are.
2. Find time each week to spend one-on-one with your teen. Take the moments when they come—and often they come late at night.
3. Address all questions honestly, even if the answer is "I don't know" or "I can't answer that now." As your child matures, the questions become harder. Be aware of times when you may need time to think before giving a response.
4. Depersonalize your teen's anger. Remember that it isn't really directed at you. Help your teen target circumstances, rules, and boundaries as the sources of his or her emotions; and be sure to apologize if you speak too quickly or harshly.
5. Listen to and validate your teen's feelings; mirror or restate those feelings, empathizing as you can; and state your opinions clearly and specifically (e.g., As your parent, it's my job to care for your safety, and I'm not comfortable with you going to a party where there will be no adult supervision.).
6. Don't get involved in power struggles. Once you've made a decision, be available to listen, but do not argue about the rightness of the rule or the responses of other kids or parents. Your child has a right to have

feelings of frustration; you have the responsibility of setting safe, secure boundaries.

7. Try the "24-hour no questions asked" rule. All teens sometimes get into situations where they need help but may not feel comfortable enough to you call you. Make certain that you are there to keep your child safe. Offer to pick up your teen and his or her friends "anytime, anywhere" when they need help. Don't ask questions until the next day, after you've had time to rest and think.

8. Remember to be a resource when your teen has a problem to solve or a decision to make, but do not step in and solve the problem for him or her. (Use the six-step problem solving method that follows.)

9. Put yourself where your teen is. Be the house where kids gather.

10. Seek help if your teen
    ◆ withdraws from all friends.
    ◆ becomes disinterested in all school and church activities.
    ◆ refuses to eat or exhibits dramatic weight loss.
    ◆ has very extreme mood swings.
    ◆ makes specific threats about suicide or hurting himself/herself.
    ◆ threatens to harm you, other family members, or anyone else.

(Adapted from "Communicating with Your Teenager," FaithHome for Parents, Tony Rankin and Cynthia Ezell, Abingdon Press, 1999, pp. 3-6)

Six-Step Problem Solving Method

1. Ask your child to state the problem in his or her own words.
2. Ask your child how this problem makes him or her feel.
3. a. Have your child tell you the various choices he or she has for solving the problem.
   b. You make your suggestion.
4. a. Have your child identify the consequences of each choice.
   b. You identify the consequences of your suggestion.
5. Consider what resources are available to help solve the problem (other adults such as a teacher, coach, minister, youth pastor, relative, or a neighbor).
6. Decide what choice is best (morally right), and do it.

(Adapted from *Parenting on Point,* p. 169)

Week 3

Learning Your Child's Communication "Style"

Before Class

Background Basics

Last week we explored the developmental stages of children as they relate to communication in the home. In addition to being familiar with the specific communication skills and characteristics our children demonstrate at various ages and stages, we need to be aware of their particular communication preferences—or, in other words, their communication "style." As Jim Williams cautions in his book *Parenting on Point,* we must be careful to avoid a "one size fits all" approach when it comes to communicating with our children. He writes: "Just as children have different personality traits, they also have different communication styles.... In order to communicate more effectively, we must recognize these differences and adjust our style of communicating accordingly" (*Parenting on Point,* p. 121).

This week we will discuss two typical communication "styles" that fit most children, as well as adults. Generally speaking, we can classify our children—as well as ourselves—as being either assertive communicators or shy communicators. Though some individuals may be assertive at times and shy at other times, depending on the subject matter being discussed, most children and adults tend to fall closer to one end of the spectrum than the other. Let's take a look at each of these two communication "styles" or personalities.

The Shy Child

The shy child is generally reluctant to share his or her feelings. This child may have been born shy, or may have become shy after having some bad experiences in sharing his or her feelings. In either case, the shy child tends to keep his or her feelings inside. To communicate most effectively with your shy child, you will need to meet your child in his or her "comfort zone." For most children, their comfort zone is their bedroom. Many shy children spend a lot of time in their rooms with the door closed. They do this because this is where they feel safe and secure. According to Jim Williams, "This is why experts agree that one of the best places to have a meaningful conversation with the [shy] child—or any child, for that matter—is in the child's bedroom" (*Parenting on Point*, p. 122-23).

Another "comfort zone" for a shy child might be a tree house, a playhouse, a fort, or some other place that gives the child a feeling of comfort and security. As Jim Williams points out, the place isn't important; what's important is identifying where your child feels most comfortable "so that you may talk together without any barriers to hinder the flow of words or hide his or her true feelings" (*Parenting on Point*, p. 123). Though your child's comfort zone certainly isn't the *only* place where you can communicate effectively with your shy child, it is an extremely important place for those planned one-on-one conversations that you will want to have from time to time. Remember that a shy child likes to be prepared for these special conversations and appreciates some advance warning. Williams suggests that you tell your shy child you'd like to talk later in his or her room, and that you even take along some cookies to reinforce your love and care for your child.

Of course, regular communication about everyday activities and interests is also important to your shy child. These kinds of conversations should take place daily and can happen in the car, at the kitchen table, in the family room, or anywhere you and your child happen to be. Find your own times and ways to "draw out" your shy child on a regular basis. Parents with young children find that playtime and story time are good opportunities for talking and "connecting." Parents of older children often take advantage of "talk time" in the car while going to and from practices and lessons. The important thing is to look for opportunities to initiate conversation with your shy child wherever and whenever you can.

Though you will be the one initiating conversation much of time, there also will be times when your shy child will seek you out. Jim Williams advises that whenever this happens, "treat this occasion as something special and give the child your full and undivided attention" (*Parenting on Point*, p. 124). He also advises that you save all meaningful or in-depth conversations with your spouse until after the children have gone to bed so that your children may approach you freely. Regardless of who initiates the conversation, be sure to tailor *your* approach to meet the needs of your shy child. See Tools and Tips (p. 39-40) for some specific suggestions for communicating with your shy child.

The Assertive Child

Unlike the shy child, the assertive child is eager to share his or her feelings—and does so without hesitation! Your assertive child isn't afraid of talking with you and doesn't need to be "drawn out." In fact, he or she usually seeks you out whenever he or she needs to talk about something. It may seem that your assertive child is *always* ready to talk—often at inopportune times. If you're busy and tell your assertive child to come back in ten minutes, chances are that he or she will be back in five minutes. When this happens, Jim Williams advises that sending the child away for another five minutes is not a good idea. Instead, he suggests that when your assertive child comes to you the second time, stop what you're doing and give him or her your undivided attention. "Though an assertive child is less easily discouraged than a nonassertive child," he explains, "it *is* possible to eventually discourage the assertive child; and once you do, he or she will quit coming back to you...." (*Parenting on Point,* p. 126).

So, despite the frequency of your assertive child's communication, it is important for you to remain accessible. Again, it's advisable to postpone meaningful or in-depth conversations with your spouse until after your child has gone to bed. Although you won't have to be as intentional about daily communication with your assertive child as you might need to be with a shy child, that everyday communication is equally important; so be open to everyday opportunities for communicating with your assertive child, and make the most of them.

Of course, there will be times when you will be the one initiating communication, especially when you need to discuss a serious or sensitive issue. At these times, you will find that your assertive child is no different than a shy child: Your child is more approachable and comfortable in his or her comfort zone. Even assertive children are more attentive and receptive when they feel at ease. As we've already seen, the number one comfort zone for most children is their bedroom. *Your* child's comfort zone is wherever he or she feels most secure and comfortable.

Whenever and wherever you talk with your assertive child, be sure to tailor your approach to meet the needs of your unique child. See Tools and Tips (p. 40) for some specific suggestions for communicating with your assertive child.

Knowing Your Child...and Yourself

Though most children—and adults—generally tend to be either shy or assertive when it comes to communication, we must remember that people are as unique as their fingerprints. Therefore, we need to pay close attention to our children's unique differences, as well as to our own unique communication characteristics. As Jim Williams points out, some children are assertive on the ball field yet are shy when it comes to talking. The categories we commonly use to describe our children's personalities—compliant, strong-willed, and rebellious—do not always correspond to their communication styles. A child can actually be nonassertive in his or her behavior and assertive in his or her communication. Another child might be assertive in his or her behavior and shy in his or her communication. Jim Williams observes:

> Every child is a complex human being with ever-changing needs. Sometimes a child simply wants someone to listen and give a hug. Other times that same child needs more assertive feedback or requests. So, if you have concluded that communicating with children can be a confusing and difficult venture, you're right. It's not a lost cause, however! All it takes is a little observation and the willingness to adapt your approach to meet the needs of *your unique child*. (*Parenting on Point,* p. 129)

In order to understand our children's communication "styles" better—as well as our own—and, therefore, be able to adapt our approach to meet their needs, we must spend more time talking with our children. In addition to being intentional about communicating with your children on a daily basis, plan to have an extended "talk time" with each child every week. This should be a time for one-on-one conversation without interruptions or distractions—ideally, one hour with each child weekly. Many parents often find the weekend to be a good time for this. Whether you choose to do something special with your child or simply to take the child along with you on a walk or an errand, this time together will do wonders for encouraging genuine sharing and relationship building. There's no better way to get to know your child and his or her preferred "style" or way of communicating than spending time alone together. Try it this week!

During Class

In Focus

The purpose of this session is to help you recognize and understand two typical communication "styles" or personalities that fit most children, and to help you identify the unique communication style of each of your own children so that you may begin tailoring your approach in communicating with your children to meet their specific needs.

Wisdom from the Word

Be devoted to each other like a loving family. Excel in showing respect for each other. (Romans 12:10 God's Word Translation)

Opening Prayer

Dear God, thank you for making us all so different and giving us unique personalities. It's not always easy to get along with those who are different from us, especially when we live with them day in and day out. Help us to better understand the unique personalities of our children and the ways they communicate with us; and teach us to change our approach as we communicate with them so that we may always meet their needs in ways that express our love and respect for the wonderful individuals they are. Amen.

Video Segment 1

Candid Kids

Running Time: 2:03 minutes

Discussion Questions

1. Did you gain any insights from the children's comments?
2. Was there one comment that caught your attention more than others?

Video Segment 2

A Parent's Perspective

Running Time: 9:15 minutes

Group Discussion

1. Read aloud this week's Wisdom from the Word (page 37). How can understanding your child's communication personality help you to fulfill this verse?
2. What do you consider the greatest challenge in communicating with a shy or non-assertive child? What insight related to communicating with the shy child do you believe will be most helpful to you?
3. What do you consider the greatest challenge in communicating with an assertive child? What insight related to communicating with the assertive child do you believe will be most helpful to you?

In Summary
Running Time: 0:40 minutes

Closing Prayer
Lord, thank you for this time of learning and fellowship. Thank you for the insights you've given us related to the unique personalities of our children and how we can be more effective in communicating with each of them. Help us to apply what we've learned as we interact with our children this week, and give us the desire and discipline to complete our homework assignments for next time. Amen.

After Class

Homework
1. Discuss the class session. What new insight(s) or understanding(s) did you gain? What do you believe will be of greatest benefit to you/your family?

_____

_____

2. Review the descriptions of the shy child and the assertive child given in Background Basics (pp. 33-35). Identify which description best fits each of your children and note any specific communication habits or preferences you've observed. Then identify any changes you need to make in your communication style or approach with each child.

Child's Name: _____

Communication "Style" and Observations: _____

_____

Changes I Need to Make: _____

Child's Name: _____

Communication "Style" and Observations: _____

_____

Changes I Need to Make: _____

Child's Name: _____

Communication "Style" and Observations: _____

_____

Changes I Need to Make: _____

Child's Name: _____

Communication "Style" and Observations: _____

_____

Changes I Need to Make: _____

3. Plan to have an extended one-on-one conversation with each child this week (ideally one hour with each child). "Schedule" these times in advance with your children, allowing them to make suggestions about when and where you will talk and what, if anything, you will do. If you like, you can keep a journal of your times together, recording things such as what you did and what you talked about, any outcomes or affects of your conversations, specific communication challenges or conflicts, and so forth. Not only will this help you to understand each child better, but it also will become a treasured keepsake of memorable moments you've spent together.

4. Read the Background Basics for Week 4.

Tools and Tips

Tips for Communicating with Your Shy Child
1. Be patient as your shy child tries to share what's on his or her mind. Sometimes "small talk" can help your child open up and move on to deeper feelings or issues.
2. Because a shy child tends to say less than an assertive child, it's often tempting to make assumptions, which may or may not be accurate, and jump to conclusions. Avoid this temptation! Actively listen to what your child is saying and "translate" or restate what you hear to avoid any misunderstanding.

3. Try not to dominate the conversation or fill the silence, but allow your child as much time as he or she needs to speak. As you listen, remember to take off your "sunglasses" (your life experiences that color the way you see the world) and see things through your child's eyes.
4. Be intentional about asking your child how he or she feels; then share your feelings as well. Always remember to express disappointment rather than anger.
5. If your child has a problem that needs to be solved, remember to walk your child through the six-step problem solving method rather than solving the problem for your child (see p. 32).
6. Always end the conversation with words that encourage and affirm your child of your love and care.

Tips for Communicating with Your Assertive Child

1. Remember that despite your assertive child's exterior, he or she has the same emotions and sensitive feelings on the inside as any shy child has. After all, children are children. Your assertive child needs to be reassured of your love, too. In fact, often an assertive child's behavior is a "cry" for that reassurance.
2. As Jim Williams points out, "Sometimes we tend to wear our 'kid gloves' when communicating with our nonassertive children and 'boxing gloves' when communicating with our assertive children!" (Parenting on Point, p. 128). Don't allow your assertive child's "in your face" communication style to make you confrontational. Take off those boxing gloves and, while you're at it, take off your "sunglasses" as well. Try to see things from your child's point of view.
3. Because an assertive child tends to say more than a shy child, it's often tempting to interrupt and interject your own thoughts and feelings. Avoid this temptation! Practice active listening, allowing your child to fully express himself or herself. Restate what your child has said to be sure you understand before responding.
4. Listen without responding as your assertive child expresses how he or she feels; validate your child's feelings before sharing your own. Always remember to express disappointment rather than anger.
5. If your child has a problem, remember to walk your child through the six-step problem solving method (see p. 32) rather than trying to solve the problem for your child or, equally harmful, letting your assertive child make decisions without any parental guidance. Even strong-willed assertive children need to be taught how to solve problems for themselves.
6. As with any child, whether shy or assertive, always end the conversation with words that encourage and affirm your child of your love and care.

Week 4

Improving Communication in Your Home

Before Class

Background Basics

As we learned in Week 1, most of us build barriers that keep us from being good listeners—barriers such as the "problem personalities" we assume and the ineffective listening habits we practice. Recognizing and removing these barriers is an important first step to improving communication in our homes. We also learned that in addition to removing these barriers, we must build "bridges" if we want to become better listeners and communicators. These bridges will help us move from poor listening to attentive listening and, finally, to effective or active listening, which is the highest level of listening. According to Jim Williams, becoming an effective or active listener should be the goal of every parent.

In Week 1 we saw that the S-P-E-A-K strategy can be a helpful bridge to effective communication:

S – Speak the truth in love.
P – Permit all feelings to be expressed.
E – Educate yourself about your child's developmental stages.
A – Actively listen.
K – Know your children and yourself.

We considered the importance of educating ourselves about our children's developmental stages (the "E") in Week 2. Then, in Week 3, we explored the need to know our children's unique communication "styles," as well as our own (the "K"). This week we'll mention the other steps of the S-P-E-A-K strategy—the "S," "P," and "A"—as we look closely at three specific habits that will help us to become effective listeners and communicators.

Habit # 1: Take off your sunglasses and translate what you hear.

As Jim Williams points out, we tend to wear our "sunglasses" when we listen to others, especially our children. In other words, we see their world through our life experiences, which shades what we hear them saying. Our sunglasses keep our focus on ourselves rather than on our children, making it very difficult for us to express our love and care for them. We wear our sunglasses with our children when we "give them the third degree" to satisfy our needs rather than theirs, when we express our feelings before we give them a chance to express theirs, when we make assumptions or draw conclusions based on what we think they've said, and other times when we allow our experiences to "shade" or color what we hear them saying. We take off our sunglasses when we stop these negative habits and begin to actively listen to our children—"translating" rather than "interpreting" what they say.

How is translating different from interpreting? Translating is clearly understanding and communicating what others are saying. It involves listening attentively and restating what you hear, asking for verification or clarification. Jim Williams suggests we restate in another way what our children are saying as if we're translating what they're saying from one language into another. When we practice translating, we hold our own opinions and thoughts on the matter until we're sure we understand accurately. Only then are we able to offer an accurate and helpful response. This is a time when the "S" of the S-P-E-A-K strategy comes into play—speaking the truth in love. Only when we realize what our children are truly saying are we able to give them the understanding and help they need. Translating tells our children that we care about them and their feelings and want to see things from their perspective.

Unfortunately, translating doesn't come naturally. As you'll remember from Week 1, we all have the need to be understood, which causes us to focus on what *we* have to say rather than on what the other person is saying. As parents, we're eager to share our knowledge with our children, and we often respond before we've taken the time to understand their point of view. Our children see this as either our unwillingness or our inability to understand them.

The good news is that we *can* change! With practice, we all can learn to take off our sunglasses and retrain ourselves to translate rather than interpret. When we do, our children not only feel loved and understood, but they also are more inclined to confide in us in the future.

Habit #2: Be attentive to your children.

Learning to give our children our undivided attention is another important habit we must acquire if we want to become effective listeners and improve the communication in our homes. A key aspect of being attentive to our children is learning to listen attentively. Attentive listening is especially important when a child is upset and is openly expressing his or her feelings. In their book *How to Talk to Kids So Kids Will Listen and Listen So Kids Will Talk,* Adele Faber and Elaine Mazlish offer some tips for becoming an attentive listener, such as...

◆ Listen quietly, acknowledging your children's feelings with simple words such as "Oh, I see."
◆ Give your children's feelings a name, such as saying, "That sounds frustrating," or "That must make you feel sad."
◆ Avoid making unhelpful responses such as blaming or accusing; giving threats, warnings, or commands; moralizing; making comparisons; and using sarcasm.
◆ Acknowledge your children's feelings rather than tell them you know how they feel.

Translating, which we discussed previously, is also a part of attentive listening.

In addition to listening attentively, there are other ways we can be attentive to our children, such as being aware of body language, tone of voice, and facial expressions—both theirs and ours. To ensure we give our children our undivided attention, Jim Williams suggests we turn off the radio, TV, or any other mechanical noises. Then, without any distractions, we can "tune in" to what our children are saying verbally as well as nonverbally. According to experts, much of our children's communication is conveyed through body language. In fact, children under the age of ten communicate 80 percent of the time through body language. Maintaining good eye contact also plays an important role in effective nonverbal communication.

Perhaps one of the most important aspects of being an attentive parent is simply being available and interested in your child. Jim Williams calls this "staying on the inside." Staying on the inside means that we make ourselves available to our children, even at inopportune times and times when their emotional eruptions are irritating or uncomfortable to us, which we'll discuss in greater detail in the next habit. If we want to stay "in the loop" with our children, we must acquire the habit of being attentive.

Habit #3: Practice the skill of lightly probing.

One of the most effective skills or habits a parent can learn is called lightly probing. It is this habit that moves us from attentive listening to the highest level of listening, which is effective or active listening; and it is here that the "A" of the S-P-E-A-K strategy comes into play: actively listen. Remember the "problem personalities" we discussed in Week 1? Both the Drill Sergeant and Prosecuting Attorney know how to probe, but neither one does it *lightly*! Lightly probing is asking questions in a gentle, non-threatening way. This approach helps to remove some of the "layers" that keep our children's feelings from surfacing.

Let's say that your child comes home from school, and her body language tells you that she had a bad day. You ask what kind of day she had, and she says it was fine. Rather than accepting her response, you ask her to tell you about what she did at school, how a certain subject or class went, or what things were like with her friends. In other words, you try to keep the conversation from ending. If she still refuses to talk, then you make a mental note to come back to the subject later, perhaps at bedtime.

As Jim Williams explains, lightly probing helps you to penetrate into your child's deeper emotions. It helps you not only to clarify how your child is feeling, but also to keep the focus on your child. Rather than telling your child how *you* would feel if you were in your child's shoes, you ask non-threatening questions that allow your child to express how he or she is feeling. Likewise, rather than giving unwanted advice or solving the problem for your child, you walk your child through the six-step problem solving method discussed in Week 3 (see p. 32). If you want to "stay on the inside" of your children's lives, lightly probing is one of the best ways to help your children "open up" and share their innermost feelings.

Jim Williams observes that, in general, mothers tend to be better at allowing children to express their feelings because they enjoy listening and aren't afraid of being exposed to their children's messy, complicated, or painful emotions. He writes:

> We want our children to share their innermost feelings with us, and yet sometimes we react in such a negative manner that our children feel it's safer to keep their feelings inside. No matter how angry or frustrated they can make us feel by sharing the truth with us, we are always far better off when our children feel they can share their true feelings with us. (*Parenting on Point*, p. 138)

This is where the "P" of the S-P-E-A-K strategy is relevant: permitting all feelings to be expressed. Likewise, it is another instance when you can practice the "S" strategy—speaking the truth in love. If you will learn to lightly probe and permit your children to express *all* of their feelings—regardless of how uncomfortable or frustrated those feelings may make *you* feel—you will truly understand your children and, therefore, be able to respond in a way that is not only helpful but also compassionate and loving. And that will go a long, long way toward improving the communication in your home.

During Class

In Focus

The purpose of this session is to give you some specific and practical habits you can adopt in order to make significant and lasting improvements in the communication in your home.

Wisdom from the Word

Listen, for I have worthy things to say. (Proverbs 8:6 NIV)

Opening Prayer

Dear God, we sincerely want to improve the communication in our homes, and yet it's so difficult to change our own bad habits when it comes to listening and speaking to our children. Give us wisdom today as we explore some specific ways we can replace our bad habits with good ones, and give us the desire and the determination to make these habits permanent. We acknowledge that we can't do it alone; we need you to empower us. Thank you, Lord. Amen.

Video Segment 1

Candid Kids
Running Time: 1:47 minutes

1. Did you gain any insights from the children's comments?
2. Was there one comment that caught your attention more than others?

Video Segment 2

A Parent's Perspective
Running Time: 13:40 minutes

Group Discussion
1. Read aloud this week's Wisdom from the Word (page 45). When communicating with your children, do you tend to be more interest-

ed in what your child has to say or in what you have to say? In what ways can you demonstrate to your child that you believe he or she has worthy things to say?

2. What does it mean to "take off your sunglasses" when listening to your children? Give examples. What can help you to do this?

3. Discuss the techniques and benefits of the following effective communication strategies:
   ◆ translating what your children are saying
   ◆ "lightly probing"
   ◆ teaching your children the skill of problem solving (which involves offering advice only when asked)

Video Segment 3

In Summary
Running Time: 0:40 minutes

Closing Prayer
Lord, thank you for this time of learning and fellowship. Thank you for the insights you've given us related to ways we can improve the communication in our homes. Help us to apply what we've learned as we communicate with our children this week, and help us to complete our final homework assignments. Amen.

After Class

Homework
1. Discuss the class session. What new insight(s) or understanding(s) did you gain? What do you believe will be of greatest benefit to you/your family?

_____

_____

2. For the first half of the week, try to identify the way(s) you most often wear your "sunglasses" when listening to your children. Do you ask too many questions before listening? Do you express your own feelings before giving them a chance to express theirs? Do you tend to make assumptions or jump to conclusions? Do you allow your own life expe

riences to color what you hear them saying? Note your observations below:

_____

_____

3. For the second half of the week, practice translating what your children are saying before responding. Does this help you to "speak the truth in love"—to give your children the understanding and help they need while expressing your love and care? If not, what else do you think might help you to take off your sunglasses and see things from your children's point of view?

_____

_____

_____

4. How attentive are you? Rate yourself by choosing one of the following qualifiers for each statement below. Write the appropriate number in the blank provided.

always (3)   mostly (2)   sometimes (1)   never(0)

_____ I translate what my children are saying (restate it in another way) and make sure I've understood before responding.

_____ I acknowledge my children's feelings, rather than tell them I know how they feel, using simple words such as "Oh, I see."

_____ I give my children's feelings a name, such as saying, "That sounds frustrating," or "That must make you sad."

_____ I ask questions in a gentle, non-threatening way in order to clarify my children's true feelings.

_____ I avoid making unhelpful responses such as blaming or accusing; giving threats, warnings, or commands; moralizing; making comparisons; or using sarcasm.

_____ I "stay on inside" by making myself available to my children, even at inopportune times and times when their emotional eruptions are irritating or uncomfortable to me.

What's your "score"?

0-6   You tend to wear your "sunglasses" when listening to your children. Be intentional this week to focus on your children and their

_____

feelings—rather than on you and your feelings—as you listen to them. Try to see things from their point of view.

7-12 You're on your way to becoming an attentive listener. Though you sometimes forget to take off your "sunglasses," you generally try to see things from your children's point of view and understand how they feel. Keep practicing taking your sunglasses off and trying to put yourself in your children's shoes. Identify the specific skills you're weak in and focus on those this week.

13-18 Congratulations! You're an attentive listener. Before you give yourself permission to "relax," however, remember that none of us is perfect. There's always room for improvement. Besides, our children are changing every day, which means that our relationships must continue to change. Just when you think you've figured out how to communicate with your child, he or she will throw you a curve ball. Stay prepared by regularly "practicing" the skills of attentive listening and paying attention to each child and the changing dynamics of your relationship.

Tools and Tips

12 Ways to Improve Communication in Your Home

1. Recognize that children have different communication styles, and be adaptable in order to meet each child's needs.
2. Increase and optimize everyday communication opportunities with all family members (mealtimes, morning/bedtime routines, car time, phone calls, shared activities, etc.). Keep a communication log your bedside table, and each night write down how many minutes you spent talking one-on-one with each of your children that day. Note how many of those minutes were uplifting and included words of praise.
3. Have an extended "one-on-one" (at least one hour) with every member of the family once a week. (The weekend is often a good time for this.)
4. Meet your child in his or her comfort zone (often the child's bedroom) for serious or meaningful conversations. Remember to give advance warning and turn off distractions such as the TV, radio, cell phones, and so forth.
5. Be accessible and attentive to your children, listening when they want to tell you something.
6. Practice effective or active listening by taking off your "sunglasses" and translating what your child is saying (restating in another way what you've heard), lightly probing to clarify and name your child's feelings,

paying attention to both your child's and your own body language, and communicating your genuine interest, love, and care for your child.

7. Try to save meaningful conversations with your spouse, or another adult, until after the children have gone to bed.

8. Set aside one hour for a family quiet time each week (no mechanical noise allowed). If possible, do this on the same day and at the time each week for continuity. During this hour, be attentive to the desires of your children. Remember, this is not a time for individual pursuits but for family interaction.

9. Have weekly family meetings (not to exceed one hour) followed by a fun family activity. This is a time for reviewing the previous week's activities, planning the activities for the coming week, and discussing any concerns or conflicts. This is an excellent opportunity for teaching your children how to compromise.

10. Have regular family dinners and other activities that involve the entire family.

11. Reduce the stress in your own life.

12. If at all possible, try to make arrangements so that one parent is home when the children get home from school. This is one of the best opportunities for listening to your children.
(Adapted from *Parenting on Point,* pp. 130-131)

---

10 Ways to "Stay on the Inside" of Your Child's Life

1. Make yourself available to listen. Look for these and other listening opportunities:
   - Eat together at mealtime.
   - Help your child with his or her homework.
   - Watch TV together.
   - Drive your children to their various activities.
   - Be a "gathering house." Let your children invite their friends to your house.

2. Don't let your child's anger fuel your anger. Remember to express your disapproval of your child's behavior while affirming your love for your child. Find out what's behind your child's anger and address the real issue. Help your child direct angry feelings at causes or situations, not people.

3. Always try to maintain a pleasant, respectful tone of voice.

4. Never belittle your child's feelings. Instead, allow your child to express all of his or her feelings, acknowledging and naming them with simple words.

5. Don't overreact to your child's emotional "eruptions." Anticipate them

by listening, watching, and waiting; then embrace them, viewing them as opportunities for uncovering your child's deeper feelings and strengthening your relationship.

6. Practice effective or active listening skills, such as translating, lightly probing, being aware of body language, and guiding your child through the six-step problem solving method (see p. 32).

7. Be aware of your body language. For example, avoid crossing your arms, and always maintain good eye contact.

8. Never dominate a conversation; let your child know that you truly want to hear what he or she has to say.

9. Encourage and allow respectful discussion and debate. However, whenever core values are in question, reinforce your point of view by making references and connections to your family's value system. In time, your child will come to realize that there are certain issues that are nonnegotiable.

10. Create an environment of love, trust, and support in your home.

(Adapted from *Parenting on Point, pp.137-138; 141*)